FREEDOM'S PROMISE

THE HARLEM
RENAISSANCE

BY DUCHESS HARRIS, JD, PHD
WITH MARTHA LONDON

Cover image: King Oliver's Creole Jazz Band was popular in the 1920s.

Core Library

An Imprint of Abdo Publishing
abdobooks.com

abdobooks.com

Published by Abdo Publishing, a division of ABDO, PO Box 398166,
Minneapolis, Minnesota 55439. Copyright © 2020 by Abdo Consulting
Group, Inc. International copyrights reserved in all countries. No part of this
book may be reproduced in any form without written permission from the
publisher. Core Library™ is a trademark and logo of Abdo Publishing.

Printed in the United States of America, North Mankato, Minnesota
092019
012020

Cover Photo: Stefano Bianchetti/Corbis Historical/Getty Images
Interior Photos: Stefano Bianchetti/Corbis Historical/Getty Images, 1; Michael Ochs Archives/
Getty Images, 5; Bettmann/Getty Images, 6–7, 8, 43; Shutterstock Images, 11; akg-images/
Newscom, 14–15; Siegfried Pilz/United Archives/Roba/Newscom, 18; Red Line Editorial, 20;
Eric Schwab/AFP/Getty Images, 22–23; Richard B. Levine/Newscom, 24; Schomburg Center for
Research in Black Culture/New York Public Library, 30–31; AP Images, 33; Stanley Wolfson/Everett
Collection/Newscom, 36–37

Editor: Maddie Spalding
Series Designer: Ryan Gale

Library of Congress Control Number: 2019942112

Publisher's Cataloging-in-Publication Data

Names: Harris, Duchess, author. | London, Martha, author.
Title: The Harlem renaissance / by Duchess Harris and Martha London
Description: Minneapolis, Minnesota : Abdo Publishing, 2020 | Series: Freedom's promise |
    Includes online resources and index.
Identifiers: ISBN 9781532190827 (lib. bdg.) | ISBN 9781532176678 (ebook)
Subjects: LCSH: Harlem Renaissance, 1920-1940--Juvenile literature. | New Negro Movement--
    Juvenile literature. | Harlem (New York, N.Y.)--Intellectual life--20th century--Juvenile
    literature. | Arts, Modern--20th century--Juvenile literature. | African American arts--
    Juvenile literature.
Classification: DDC 700.899--dc23

CONTENTS

A LETTER FROM DUCHESS

The Harlem Renaissance is one of the most-taught units in schools. I wondered for years why this movement was so important. In simple terms, Black Americans used art, literature, and music to demand equality.

Black Americans faced widespread violence and discrimination in the South. Many fled north in the early 1900s to escape these threats. Some settled in Harlem, a neighborhood in New York City. They expressed themselves and their experiences through music, art, and writing. They celebrated their heritage and cultures in their work. At a time when white Americans continued to oppress Black Americans, Harlem Renaissance activists promoted racial pride.

This book introduces you to influential Harlem Renaissance writers, artists, and musicians. It also shows the challenges they faced in their fight for equality. Please join me on a journey to learn about a movement that provided artistic and literary freedom.

Duchess Harris

Harlem, New York City, was known for its ballrooms and nightclubs in the 1920s.

SWINGING AT THE SAVOY

I t was past 11:00 p.m. on a spring night in 1931. The neighborhood of Harlem, New York City, was just waking up. Harlem came alive after dark. Well-dressed men and women walked down the sidewalk. The women wore dresses and heels. The men wore suits. The crowd headed toward the flashing lights of the Savoy Ballroom. Duke Ellington and his jazz band were playing at the Savoy. Ellington was a pianist and composer.

Many people who lived in Harlem worked in factories. After a long day of work, they came to the Savoy to relax and have fun.

Trumpeter Cootie Williams plays at Harlem's Savoy Ballroom in the 1930s.

The Savoy Ballroom could hold up to 4,000 people.

In the lobby, a huge glass chandelier hung from the ceiling. Men and women talked in the open space. They listened to the music filtering in from the ballroom.

The ballroom's wood floor was nearly as long as a football field. At the far end, two bands sat on a stage.

The second band started playing after Ellington's band finished a set. The ballroom always had music.

Black and white people danced on the floor. Some dancers practiced the Lindy Hop. The Lindy Hop was a type of partner dance. It had fast footwork. The Savoy was always lively and full of dancers. Because of this, many people called it the Home of Happy Feet.

People from all over New York came to the Savoy for the music and dancing. It was one of the most popular ballrooms on Manhattan Island. Unlike other clubs and ballrooms in New York,

PERSPECTIVES

NORMA MILLER

Norma Miller was an African American dancer. She was born in Manhattan in 1919. She grew up in Harlem. She danced the Lindy Hop at the Savoy. People enjoyed watching her dance. Because of her swing-dancing talent, many people called her the Queen of Swing. In an interview, Miller talked about her experiences at the Savoy. She said, "We didn't have segregation at the Savoy. The Savoy opened the doors for all people being together."

the Savoy was bright and airy. Other places were dark and full of smoke. The Savoy was also integrated. Black couples and white couples shared the dance floor. Integration was unusual in the 1930s. Most restaurants and clubs were still segregated. White club and restaurant owners did not want Black people to interact with white people. Many places banned Black people.

A NEW RENAISSANCE

In the early 1900s, Harlem's population was growing. Many Black artists and writers lived in the neighborhood. African American art, literature, and music flourished in Harlem. Soon many people throughout the country embraced Black arts and culture. Historians call this period the Harlem Renaissance.

Many of Harlem's residents came from the South. African Americans faced widespread racism and violence in the South. Southern lawmakers had created strict segregation laws called Jim Crow laws. These laws

MAP OF
HARLEM

This map shows the neighborhood of Harlem in New York City. Harlem is 3.1 square miles (8 sq km) in size. How does the map help you better understand the area where the Harlem Renaissance took place?

New Jersey

Hudson River

The Bronx

Harlem

Harlem River

Manhattan

N
W E
S

separated Black people from white people. Black people could not use the same services and facilities as white people. For example, they could not attend the same schools. Many African Americans moved from the South to New York City and other places in the North. They hoped to find more acceptance and opportunities in the North.

ELLA FITZGERALD

Ella Fitzgerald was a well-known figure during the Harlem Renaissance. She was a popular jazz singer. Today, many people consider her to be one of the greatest singers of all time. In 1934 Fitzgerald won a talent contest at the Apollo Theatre in New York City. She was just 17 years old. She later joined a band. She sang regularly at the Savoy. She recorded more than 2,000 songs in her lifetime.

African Americans found and created their own communities in northern cities. With this urban population boom came a new culture. The Harlem Renaissance was a time of growing racial pride. Black art, music, and writing had political messages. Black artists promoted civil rights in their work. The Harlem Renaissance set the stage for the American civil rights movement as African Americans began demanding equality.

The work of Black artists, writers, and musicians became more popular among white people during the Harlem Renaissance. But racial tensions were still high. Segregation and discrimination followed Black Americans northward. Black artists and activists protested this mistreatment. Today, the Harlem Renaissance is recognized as one of the most important periods of African American history.

FURTHER EVIDENCE

Chapter One introduces the Harlem Renaissance. What is one of the main points of this chapter? What key evidence supports this point? Go to the article at the website below. Does the information on the website support this point? Or does it present new evidence?

WHAT WAS THE HARLEM RENAISSANCE?
abdocorelibrary.com/harlem-renaissance

THE GREAT MIGRATION

Beginning around 1916, many African Americans moved out of the rural South. This mass movement was called the Great Migration. African Americans migrated north and west to large cities. These cities needed workers after World War I (1914–1918) broke out. Cities in the West and North had large factories. These factories made war supplies.

Jim Crow laws pushed many African Americans out of the South. Black people also left the South to escape poverty. One of the only jobs available to Black people was sharecropping. Sharecroppers rented land that

Some African American women sewed military uniforms in factories during World War I.

they farmed. In return for use of the land, they gave the landowners a share of the crops at each harvest. Sharecroppers were not paid very much for their work. Their situation worsened in 1910. An insect called the boll weevil ate many crops in the South. This was a huge loss for sharecroppers. Their harvests suffered. Many lost their jobs. They had to look for new work. They moved north in the hope of finding better jobs.

RACE RIOTS

During World War I, many white working men left their jobs to serve abroad. Meanwhile, it became harder for people from Europe to immigrate to the United States.

NOT JUST HARLEM

The Great Migration affected many cities across the United States. In addition to Harlem, several cities experienced cultural revolutions. These cities included Cleveland, Ohio, and Los Angeles, California. Black musicians toured through or settled permanently in these cities. Harlem became a kind of capital for Black artists. But the cultural awakening created by the Great Migration spread throughout most major US cities.

Many factories had previously hired immigrants. African Americans now filled those empty positions. Some Black people moved into majority-white neighborhoods in northern cities. Many white people disliked this. They did not want to live near Black people.

After the war ended, white soldiers came back to the United States. They wanted their old jobs back. White people saw Black people as competition for employment. As a result, tensions increased. These tensions sometimes led to riots.

In 1917 a riot broke out in Saint Louis, Missouri. Freda Josephine McDonald was 11 years old at the time. She lived in Saint Louis with her family. She saw white people burn down Black people's homes. The rioters injured and killed many Black people.

African Americans fled the South to escape such violence. Some gained fame and success during the Harlem Renaissance. Freda moved to New York City when she was 13 years old. She married at the age

Harlem Renaissance dancer Josephine Baker was known for her style and elaborate costumes.

of 15. She took her husband's last name and became Josephine Baker. She gained fame as a dancer. She left New York after a few years and moved to Paris, France. She became a popular dancer there too.

MOVING TO HARLEM

Like Baker, many African Americans moved north to escape violence. The Great Migration lasted more than 50 years. From 1916 to 1970, approximately 6 million African Americans left the South.

By 1920, nearly 175,000 African Americans had moved to Harlem. Harlem was originally meant to be a neighborhood for rich white people. But some houses sat empty. Black people bought these houses. Black people were drawn to Harlem because it was close to job opportunities in New York City.

At first, white Harlem residents tried to keep Black people out. They thought Black people were poor and uneducated. But racism did not keep Black people away. More Black people came to the neighborhood.

PERSPECTIVES
LANGSTON HUGHES

Langston Hughes was a poet during the Harlem Renaissance. He believed artists should create art that reflects their experiences. He encouraged Black artists to be proud of their racial heritage. In 1926 he wrote an essay called "The Negro Artist and the Racial Mountain." In it, he wrote: "We younger Negro artists who create now intend to express our individual dark-skinned selves without fear or shame. If white people are pleased we are glad. If they are not, it doesn't matter. We know we are beautiful."

HARLEM'S BLACK POPULATION

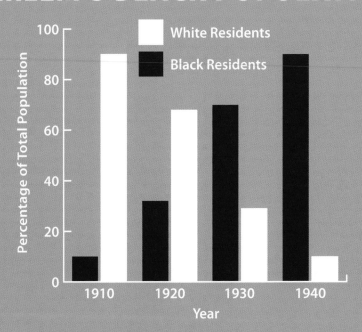

White Residents
Black Residents

Percentage of Total Population

100 — 80 — 60 — 40 — 20 — 0

1910   1920   1930   1940

Year

This graph shows the racial makeup of Central Harlem over time. What trend do you notice? How quickly did Harlem's Black population grow?

They created their own community. As African Americans arrived, white people left.

Before the Great Migration, most African Americans did not live close together. In the South, many African Americans lived on farms. The farms were often far away from each other. But in Harlem, Black people were neighbors. This environment brought artists and activists together. They influenced each other.

STRAIGHT TO THE
SOURCE

Dorothy West was a writer during the Harlem Renaissance. She grew up in Boston, Massachusetts. She later moved to Harlem. In an interview, she described her first impressions of Harlem and New York:

> My mother told us . . . that New York was not like Boston—they were real prejudiced, and so on, and warned us all about that. We went on the subway, and got off in Harlem. And there were all these colored people all over the place. . . .
>
> Of course, we fell, as everybody does, in love with New York. . . . We were all the same age, and we all had the same ambitions—writers or painters or so forth. We had all come from small towns. We were free.

Source: Danica Kirka. "Dorothy West: A Voice of Harlem Renaissance Talks of Past—But Values the 'Now.'" *Los Angeles Times.* Los Angeles Times. January 1, 1995. Web. Accessed June 7, 2019.

Point of View

West's first impression of Harlem was positive. What are some of the reasons she gives for this reaction? Read back through this chapter. Do you think other Black people might have had similar experiences when they came to Harlem? Why or why not?

ARTS AND ENTERTAINMENT

In the 1920s, jazz music became popular throughout the United States. This period is known as the Jazz Age. Jazz is an upbeat style of music. Jazz musicians often improvise, or make up parts of songs as they play. This music defined the 1920s.

Jazz was created in Black communities in Louisiana in the late 1800s. Many jazz musicians were part of the Great Migration. Jazz flourished in big cities such as New York City. Black-owned bars and nightclubs opened in Harlem. They featured jazz music. Famous jazz

Jazz pianist Nat King Cole plays with his orchestra at the Apollo Theatre in Harlem in the 1950s.

The Lenox Lounge, opened in 1939, was a popular jazz club in Harlem.

musicians such as Louis Armstrong, Duke Ellington, and Billie Holiday performed in these places.

Many white people liked jazz. They wanted to see Black jazz musicians perform. But few of them wanted to share the space with Black guests. Whites-only nightclubs opened in some cities. The Cotton Club in Harlem was a well-known whites-only nightclub. It opened in 1922. All of the musicians and employees were African American. But none of the guests were.

Other segregated nightclubs opened. At the same time, African Americans opened Blacks-only nightclubs. There were very few integrated spaces like the Savoy. The Savoy opened in 1926.

ARTISTS

Black visual artists also found success in the 1920s. Their art, especially paintings and sculptures, gained national attention. The paintings were defined by bright, bold colors and abstract forms. Many Black artists were inspired by folk and African art. Folk art is a type of art that people pass down through generations. It reflects the artist's culture. Folk art can be sculptures or paintings. But it also includes other types of artwork, such as blankets and dishes. African art often has geometric patterns and dark lines.

When white artists drew African Americans, their depictions were often racist. Their art reflected stereotypes. For example, some artwork depicted Black people as lazy or unintelligent. Many white artists exaggerated Black people's features. They often made Black people's lips large. Black artists wanted to challenge these stereotypes. They created art that accurately represented them and their cultures. Their art depicted African Americans as strong and beautiful people. The artists encouraged Black people to be proud of their race and their heritage.

The Harlem Renaissance was a literary movement too. Black writers found success. They wrote essays, poems, novels, and plays. They also challenged popular stereotypes. White writers rarely wrote about Black people. When they did, they often used stereotypes. Black writers wanted to make their readers understand the Black experience.

Black writers encouraged activism in their work. The National Association for the Advancement of Colored People (NAACP) created its own magazine in 1910. The NAACP is a civil rights organization. Its magazine is called the *Crisis*. Black author and activist Hubert Harrison created a newspaper called the *Voice* in 1917. It covered the Harlem Renaissance. Black activists A. Philip Randolph and Chandler

ZORA NEALE HURSTON

Zora Neale Hurston was a Black writer during the Harlem Renaissance. Many people consider her to be one of the greatest writers of the 1900s. She grew up in Alabama and Florida. At the age of 16, she became part of a traveling theater company. Then she moved to New York City. She studied anthropology at Barnard College in New York City. Anthropology is the study of human cultures and societies. Hurston learned about African American folklore in the South. Her studies influenced her writing. She wrote four books and many articles. She faced discrimination. Publishers did not pay her much for her work.

Owen formed the *Messenger* magazine the same year. Black-owned magazines and newspapers such as these published Black writers' stories. Black writers wrote about the injustices African Americans faced.

THE GREAT DEPRESSION

In 1929 the US economy collapsed. Many people lost their jobs. This period was called the Great Depression. Both Black and white people had a hard time making money. The Great Depression affected countries all over the world too. During this time, the United States did not buy as many things from other countries.

Some Black artists had moved to Europe in the early 1900s to escape racial violence in the United States. During the Great Depression, many of these artists could not make much money. Some artists returned to the United States. Many settled in Harlem.

Black artists tried to stay positive in this difficult time. They inspired and encouraged other artists. For example, Black sculptor Augusta Savage created the Harlem Community Art Center. Savage offered free painting and sculpting classes. She wanted to help Black artists who were struggling. The center also employed some artists.

Art and entertainment were at the heart of the Harlem Renaissance. Even during the Great Depression, Black artists continued to create important work. Their work helped bring about social change.

EXPLORE ONLINE

Chapter Three explores the importance of art and entertainment during the Harlem Renaissance. The article at the website below goes into more depth on this topic. As you know, every source is different. What information does the website give about Harlem Renaissance art and entertainment? How is the information from the website the same as the information in Chapter Three? What new information did you learn?

THE HARLEM RENAISSANCE
abdocorelibrary.com/harlem-renaissance

A CALL TO ACTION

The Harlem Renaissance was a period of both artistic creativity and political activism. Black people acted politically when they made Harlem their symbolic capital. Black artists included political messages in their work. They addressed inequality and discrimination.

Alain Locke was a Black writer, philosopher, and educator. In 1925 he published a collection of writings by Black authors. The collection was called *The New Negro*. Today, the term "Negro" is considered offensive. But in the 1920s, some Black people

As more Black people moved into Harlem in the early 1900s, many white residents moved out.

used this term to refer to themselves. The term *New Negro* referred to a shift in the way Black people identified themselves. Locke and other writers saw that more Black people had a sense of racial pride.

DISCRIMINATION AND VIOLENCE

Across the country, Black people faced discrimination in many ways. One common form of discrimination was housing discrimination. Many white landlords wanted to keep Black people out of mostly white neighborhoods. So they refused to let Black people rent houses or apartments. White neighborhoods also created rules

In August 1943 racial tensions in Harlem erupted into a riot after a white police officer shot a Black man.

that people could not build low-income apartments. African Americans could not find affordable housing in these neighborhoods.

Redlining was another common discriminatory practice. Officials color-coded certain areas as red. These were areas where many Black people lived. Harlem was a red zone. Officials made it difficult for people in red zones to get mortgages. A mortgage is a loan. It helps people afford a home. People pay back the mortgage over time.

In the 1930s, many banks would not give Black people mortgages. They thought Black people would not make their payments on time. When banks did give

Black people mortgages, the mortgages came with high monthly payments. People who were not able to make these payments could lose their homes.

The Harlem Renaissance was a period of cultural growth. It helped launch the careers of many Black artists and writers. But in the South, conditions for Black people remained especially bad. White hate groups such as the Ku Klux Klan attacked and even killed Black people. These murders were called lynchings.

THE NAACP

In the early 1900s, activist groups such as the NAACP brought attention to the mistreatment of African Americans. Black activists founded the NAACP in New York City in 1909. The NAACP started an anti-lynching campaign. In 1917 the NAACP organized a march. Approximately 10,000 African Americans gathered in New York City. They protested lynching and racial violence.

Many Black people and some white people read the NAACP's newspaper, the *Crisis*. W. E. B. Du Bois was the newspaper's editor for many years. The newspaper published articles on many topics, including segregation and lynching. The *Crisis* was widely published. The newspaper made more people aware of the injustices and inequalities that Black people faced.

W. E. B. DU BOIS

W. E. B. Du Bois was a Black writer and editor during the Harlem Renaissance. He was also an activist. Du Bois thought the best way to bring about social change was through protest. He helped form the NAACP. He served as the editor of the NAACP's magazine, the *Crisis*, from 1910 to 1934.

The NAACP also fought housing and voting discrimination. Black people's housing options were often limited. Their voting rights were restricted too. They often had to pass a difficult test or pay a poll tax before they could register to vote. NAACP activists across the country worked to register Black voters.

MARCH SELMA

LEGACY

The Harlem Renaissance was a revolutionary period. For the first time, national publishers took Black writers seriously. Black artists and musicians became popular throughout the country. This recognition helped create racial pride for Black people in the United States. In these ways, the Harlem Renaissance helped set the stage for Pan-Africanism and the civil rights movement.

MOVEMENTS

Pan-Africanism is a movement that began in the mid-1800s. Pan-Africanists wanted to reverse the effects of colonialism. For centuries, white Europeans had colonized

Activists walk through the streets of Harlem in support of a civil rights march in Selma, Alabama, in 1965.

African countries and enslaved Africans. The slave trade was widespread. Today, descendants of enslaved people live around the world. Pan-Africanists hope to bring together people of African descent. This idea became popular during the Harlem Renaissance. Activists such as writer Richard Wright were Pan-Africanists.

Another movement that encouraged racial pride was the civil rights movement. This movement was at its peak in the 1950s and 1960s. Civil rights activists asked that

African Americans be treated the same as white people. As a result of their actions, lawmakers passed important civil rights laws. These included the Civil Rights Act of 1964 and the Fair Housing Act. The Civil Rights Act banned employment discrimination. The Fair Housing Act outlawed housing discrimination.

Other movements emerged from the civil rights movement. The Black Power Movement was created in the 1960s. It promoted racial pride and equality. Activists used direct action, such as protests, to spread the movement's message.

The Black Power Movement inspired the Black Arts Movement. Black poets such as Amiri Baraka and

CELEBRATING HARLEM

In 2018 a major celebration kicked off in Harlem. Its purpose was to remember the Harlem Renaissance. The community organized a series of events. The events were spread out over two years. Historic Harlem locations hosted African American artists and speakers. The events honored the history of Harlem and the legacy of the Harlem Renaissance.

Sonia Sanchez were involved in this movement. They were inspired by Harlem Renaissance poets. Their poetry reflected their heritage and cultural history. For example, they used African American speech patterns in their poetry. They also used jazz rhythms.

Black musicians, artists, and actors were also part of the Black Arts Movement. Their work brought attention to police violence against African Americans. Police often targeted African Americans. Police brutality is still a problem that Black activists fight today.

HARLEM TODAY

Art from the Harlem Renaissance is still widely popular today. Harlem Renaissance paintings and sculptures are preserved in museums. Radio stations play jazz artists such as Duke Ellington and Billie Holiday. The Harlem Renaissance shaped the United States in many ways. Harlem Renaissance writers and artists wanted to portray African American life truthfully. The art they created continues to influence artists and activists today.

STRAIGHT TO THE
SOURCE

Gwendolyn Brooks was a writer during the Black Arts Movement. She was a longtime friend of Langston Hughes. She described Hughes and their friendship in an article. She wrote:

The Harlem Renaissance . . . is one of the most popular subjects encountered on campuses across the country now. If a school wants to recognize blacks and blackness at all, it confronts the Harlem Renaissance. Langston Hughes was its best-loved star. . . . [He] judged blacks "the most wonderful people in the world." He wanted to celebrate them in his poetry, fiction, essays and plays. He wanted to record their strengths, their resiliency, courage, humor.

Source: Gwendolyn Brooks. "The Darker Brother." *New York Times*. New York Times. October 12, 1986. Web. Accessed June 7, 2019.

What's the Big Idea?

Take a close look at this passage. What influence does Brooks say Hughes had on the Harlem Renaissance? What does this passage tell you about Hughes's writing?

FAST FACTS

- The Great Migration describes the mass movement of millions of African Americans out of the rural South into urban areas in the North and West. This movement occurred from approximately 1916 to 1970. African Americans fled the South to escape racism and violence. They were attracted to the North and West by better job opportunities.

- Many Black migrants settled in the neighborhood of Harlem, New York City. Among them were musicians, artists, and writers. African American art and culture became widely popular in the 1920s and 1930s. This period was called the Harlem Renaissance.

- Harlem Renaissance artists promoted racial pride in their work. Much of their work was political. Many Black artists were also activists. They fought for equal treatment and an end to discrimination.

- The Harlem Renaissance set the stage for the civil rights movement and other social movements. It influenced writers and artists in the Black Arts Movement. It continues to influence Black artists and activists today.

STOP AND
THINK

Tell the Tale

Chapter One of this book explores an evening at one of Harlem's nightclubs, the Savoy Ballroom, in 1931. Imagine you are visiting the Savoy during the Harlem Renaissance. Write 200 words about your experience. What people do you meet? What music do you hear?

Dig Deeper

After reading this book, what questions do you still have about the Harlem Renaissance? With an adult's help, find a few reliable sources that can help you answer your questions. Write a paragraph about what you learned.

Why Do I Care?

The Harlem Renaissance happened approximately 100 years ago. But that doesn't mean you can't think about its influence and legacy. How does its legacy affect you? How might your life be different if the Harlem Renaissance had not happened?

GLOSSARY

colonialism
the control of one country over another country and its people

discrimination
the unjust treatment of a group of people based on their race, gender, or other characteristics

economy
a system in which goods and services are exchanged

integrate
to bring different groups of people together

racism
the belief that one race is better than others

renaissance
a resurgence or rebirth of arts and culture

rural
located in the country rather than in the city

segregation
the separation of people into groups based on race or other factors

stereotype
a common belief about a group of people that is usually negative and untrue

urban
located in or near a city

ONLINE RESOURCES

To learn more about the Harlem Renaissance, visit our free resource websites below.

Visit **abdocorelibrary.com** or scan this QR code for free Common Core resources for teachers and students, including vetted activities, multimedia, and booklinks, for deeper subject comprehension.

Visit **abdobooklinks.com** or scan this QR code for free additional online weblinks for further learning. These links are routinely monitored and updated to provide the most current information available.

LEARN MORE

Harris, Duchess, JD, PhD, with Kate Conley. *The Great Migration*. Minneapolis, MN: Abdo Publishing, 2020.

Rissman, Rebecca. *The Black Power Movement*. Minneapolis, MN: Abdo Publishing, 2015.

ABOUT THE
AUTHORS

Duchess Harris, JD, PhD

Dr. Harris is a professor of American Studies at Macalester College and curator of the Duchess Harris Collection of ABDO books. She is also the coauthor of the titles in the collection, which features popular selections such as *Hidden Human Computers: The Black Women of NASA* and series including News Literacy and Being Female in America.

Before working with ABDO, Dr. Harris authored several other books on the topics of race, culture, and American history. She served as an associate editor for *Litigation News*, the American Bar Association Section of Litigation's quarterly flagship publication, and was the first editor in chief of *Law Raza*, an interactive online journal covering race and the law, published at William Mitchell College of Law. She has earned a PhD in American Studies from the University of Minnesota and a JD from William Mitchell College of Law.

Martha London

Martha London is a writer and educator in Minnesota. When she isn't writing books for young readers, you can find her hiking in the woods.

INDEX